Birds, Beasts and Flowers

GPK

An Anthology with Illustrations

Birds, Beasts
& Flowers

as performed by
Her Serene Highness Princess Grace of Monaco

with Richard Pasco
of the Royal Shakespeare Company

Chosen by John Carroll

 *Presented at St James's Palace, London on*
22nd November 1978 in the presence of Her Majesty,
Queen Elizabeth The Queen Mother

Published in aid of the World Wildlife Fund

Webb&Bower
EXETER, ENGLAND

First published in 1981 as a
fine bound limited edition of
500 copies by
Nottingham Court Press,
44 Great Russell Street,
London WC1B 3PA

This edition published in Great Britain 1983 by
Webb & Bower (Publishers) Limited
9 Colleton Crescent, Exeter, Devon EX2 4BY

Jacket design by Les Dominey

ISBN 0 906671 93 0

Printed and bound in Italy by New Interlitho SpA.

Foreword

It has always been my hope that this very beautiful selection of poetry and prose would find a permanent record in book form.

It gives me therefore great pleasure that this edition is now being published. It is an added pleasure that this should be so on the twentieth anniversary of the founding of the World Wildlife Fund, whose work has strongly influenced the whole concept.

Those who acquire this book will I am sure derive great enjoyment from both its content and its form. They will also be contributing in a very tangible way to the work of the World Wildlife Fund.

Monaco
May, 1981

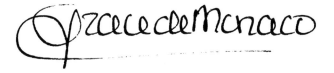

The publishers would like to thank Miss
Fleur Cowles who, as an International
Trustee of the World Wildlife Fund, has
selected the paintings and illustrations
for this edition.

Introduction

Birds, Beasts & Flowers owes its origin to an invitation received by Princess Grace from the American International Poetry Forum to give a poetry reading in the United States under their auspices.

Following the Princess's acceptance, I decided to make the selection for the programme from the themes contained in our title. Down the centuries, the world of nature has always been a source of inspiration to writers and has given us many outstanding works in both poetry and prose. Today, when we are more than ever aware of the need to protect and preserve so much of the world's wild life from massive and insidious destruction, these themes are of particular significance.

In making the selection for the reading, it was not only what went in, but also what had to be left out, because the field of choice is immense. Two further considerations were to find pieces that would suit the reader in performance and also to cover different aspects of the various themes. The choice is wide — from the King James Bible to contemporary American and English writers. A continuing link is compassion for all living things.

In its original form the programme was first presented for the International Poetry Forum at the Carnegie Hall in Pittsburgh, Pennsylvania, on the 26th and 27th February 1978, followed by a tour which included Minneapolis, Philadelphia, Washington D.C. and the universities of Princeton and Harvard.

Princess Grace had as her co-reader Richard Pasco, who also took part in the first performance of the shortened version of the programme which was specially made for presentation at St. James's Palace in London on the 22nd November 1978. This version was also presented at the Dublin Theatre Festival in

October 1979 when John Westbrook was the Princess's co-reader. It was subsequently given by Princess Grace with Richard Pasco at Tatton Park in Cheshire in February 1980. It is the shortened version which provides the selection for this anthology.

In 1855, a famous Suquamish American Indian Chief, Seatlh, after whom Seattle, Washington, is named, said words that today are even more appropriate:

'What is man without the beasts? If all the beasts were gone, man would die from great loneliness of spirit, for whatever happens to the beasts also happens to man. All things are connected.'

John Carroll
May 1981

This edition has been brought out since the tragic death of Princess Grace of Monaco, but I know that the Princess would have been glad that our anthology 'Birds, Beasts and Flowers' is now to reach a wider public and also, that the World Wildlife Fund will benefit from the new edition.

The book will therefore be another remembrance of a most beautiful and gracious lady who was always so generous in her support of the arts and of charitable causes.

J.C.

To see a World in a Grain of Sand
And a Heaven in a Wild Flower,
Hold Infinity in the palm of your hand
And Eternity in an hour.

A Robin Red breast in a Cage
Puts all Heaven in a Rage.

A Dove house fill'd with Doves & Pigeons
Shudders Hell thro' all its regions.

A Dog starv'd at his Master's Gate
Predicts the ruin of the State.

A Horse misus'd upon the Road
Calls to Heaven for Human blood.

Each outcry of the hunted Hare
A fibre from the Brain does tear.

A Skylark wounded in the wing,
A Cherubim does cease to sing.

The wild Deer wand'ring here & there
Keeps the Human Soul from Care.

He who shall hurt the little Wren
Shall never be belov'd by Men.

Joy & Woe are woven fine,
A Clothing for the Soul divine;
Under every grief & pine
Runs a joy with silken twine.

The Bleat, the Bark, Bellow & Roar
Are waves that Beat on *Heaven's* Shore.

from Auguries of Innocence, *William Blake*

BANG Bang Bang
Said the nails in the Ark.

It's getting rather dark
Said the nails in the Ark.

For the rain is coming down
Said the nails in the Ark.

And you're all like to drown
Said the nails in the Ark.

Dark and black as sin
Said the nails in the Ark.

So won't you all come in
Said the nails in the Ark.

But only two by two
Said the nails in the Ark.

So they came in two by two,
The elephant, the kangaroo,
And the gnu,
And the little tiny shrew.

Then the birds
Flocked in like wingèd words:
Two racket-tailed motmots, two macaws,
Two nuthatches and two
Little bright robins.

And the reptiles: the gila monster, the slow-worm,
The green mamba, the cottonmouth, and the alligator —
All squirmed in;
And after a *very* lengthy walk,
Two giant Galapagos tortoises.

And the insects in their hierarchies:
A queen ant, a king ant, a queen wasp, a king wasp,
A queen bee, a king bee,
And all the beetles, bugs and mosquitoes,
Cascading in like glittering, murmurous jewels.

But the fish had their wish;
For the rain came down.
People began to drown:
The wicked, the rich —
They gasped out bubbles of pure gold,
Which exhalations
Rose to the constellations.

So for forty days and forty nights
They were on the waste of waters
In those cramped quarters.
It was very dark, damp and lonely.
There was nothing to see, but only
The rain which continued to drop.
It did not stop.

So Noah sent forth a Raven. The raven said 'Kark!
I will not go back to the ark.'
The raven was footloose,
He fed on the bodies of the rich —
Rich with vitamins and goo.
They had become bloated,
And everywhere they floated.

The raven's heart was black,
He did not come back.
It was not a nice thing to do:
Which is why the raven is a token of wrath,
And creaks like a rusty gate
When he crosses your path; and Fate
Will grant you no luck that day:
The raven is fey:
You were meant to have a scare.
Fortunately in England
The raven is rather rare.

Then Noah sent forth a dove
She did not want to rove.
She longed for her love —
The other turtle dove —
(For her no other dove!)
She brought back a twig from an olive-tree.
There is no more beautiful tree
Anywhere on the earth,
Even when it comes to birth
From six weeks under the sea.

She did not want to rove.
She wanted to take her rest,
And to build herself a nest
All in the olive grove.
She wanted to make love.
She thought that was the best.

The dove was not a rover;
So they knew that the rain was over,
Noah and his wife got out
(They had become rather stout)
And Japhet, Ham, and Shem.

(The same could be said of them.)
They looked up at the sky.
The earth was becoming dry

Then the animals came ashore —
There were more of them than before:
There were two dogs and a litter of puppies;
There were a tom-cat and two tib-cats
And two litters of kittens - cats
Do not obey regulations;
And, as you might expect,
A quantity of rabbits.

God put a rainbow in the sky.
They wondered what it was for.
There had never been a rainbow before.
The rainbow was a sign;
It looked like a neon sign —
Seven colours arched in the skies:
What should it publicise?
They looked up with wondering eyes.

It advertises Mercy
Said the nails in the Ark.

Mercy Mercy Mercy
Said the nails in the Ark.

Our God is merciful
Said the nails in the Ark.

Merciful and gracious
Bang Bang Bang Bang.

John Heath-Stubbs

WHY, who makes much of a miracle?
As to me I know of nothing else but miracles,
Whether I walk the streets of Manhattan,
Or dart my sight over the roofs of houses towards the sky,
Or wade with naked feet along the beach just in the edge of
the water,
Or stand under trees in the woods, . . .

Or watch honey-bees busy around the hive of a summer
fore-noon,
Or animals feeding in the fields,
Or birds, or the wonderfulness of insects in the air,
Or the wonderfulness of the sundown, or the stars shining so
quiet and bright,
Or the exquisite delicate thin curve of the new moon in spring;
These with the rest, one and all, are to me miracles,
The whole referring, yet each distinct and in its place.

To me every hour of the light and dark is a miracle,
Every cubic inch of space is a miracle,
Every square yard of the surface of the earth is spread with the
same,
Every foot of the interior swarms with the same. . . .

from Miracles, *Walt Whitman*

Humming Bird

I CAN imagine, in some otherworld
Primeval-dumb, far back
In that most awful stillness, that only gasped and hummed,
Humming birds raced down the avenues.

Before anything had a soul,
While life was a heave of Matter, half inanimate,
This little bit chipped off in brilliance
And went whizzing through the slow, vast, succulent stems.

I believe there were no flowers then,
In the world where the humming-bird flashed ahead of creation.
I believe he pierced the slow vegetable veins with his long beak.

Probably he was big
As mosses, and little lizards, they say, were once big.
Probably he was a jabbing, terrifying monster.

We look at him through the wrong end of the long telescope
                                        of Time,
Luckily for us.

                                        D. H. Lawrence

The Tyger

TYGER, Tyger, burning bright
  In the forests of the night,
What immortal hand or eye
Could frame thy fearful symmetry?

In what distant deeps or skies
Burnt the fire of thine eyes?
On what wings dare he aspire?
What the hand dare seize the fire?

And what shoulder, & what art,
Could twist the sinews of thy heart?
And when thy heart began to beat,
What dread hand? & what dread feet?

What the hammer? what the chain,
In what furnace was thy brain?
What the anvil? what dread grasp
Dare its deadly terrors clasp?

When the stars threw down their spears
And water'd heaven with their tears,
Did he smile his work to see?
Did he who made the Lamb make thee?

Tyger, Tyger, burning bright
In the forests of the night,
What immortal hand or eye
Dare frame thy fearful symmetry?

William Blake

FLEUR-70

'IN those tropical forests where the beasts of prey roam grow many a beautiful and delicate flower.'

Mary Kingsley

The Babiaantje

HITHER, where tangled thickets of the acacia
Wreathed with a golden powder, sigh
And when the boughs grow dark, the hoopoe
Doubles his bell-like cry,
Spreading his bright striped wings and brown crest
Under a softening spring sky, —
I have returned because I cannot rest,
And would not die.

Here it was as a boy that, I remember,
I wandered ceaselessly, and knew
Sweetness of spring was in the bird's cry,
And in the hidden dew
The unbelievably keen perfume
Of the Babiaantje, a pale blue
Wild hyacinth that between narrow grey leaves
On the ground grew.

The flower will be breathing there now, should I wish
To search the grass beneath those trees,
And having found it, should go down
To sniff it, on my knees.
But now, although the crested hoopoe
Calls like a bell, how barren these
Rough ways and dusty woodlands look to one
Who has lost youth's peace!

F. T. Prince ·

WE must remember that primitive man was far closer to the animals than we can imagine. Indeed, he felt, with good reason, that the animals were his superiors. This seems to me to be the message of the early wall-paintings, like those at Lascaux. The few men who appear on the uneven walls of Lascaux cut very poor figures compared to the vigorous animals. Can we seriously believe that these wretched little creatures thought that, by representing their magnificent companions, they were gaining power over them? Are they not, rather, expressing their envy and admiration?

Animals and Men, *Kenneth Clark*, 1977

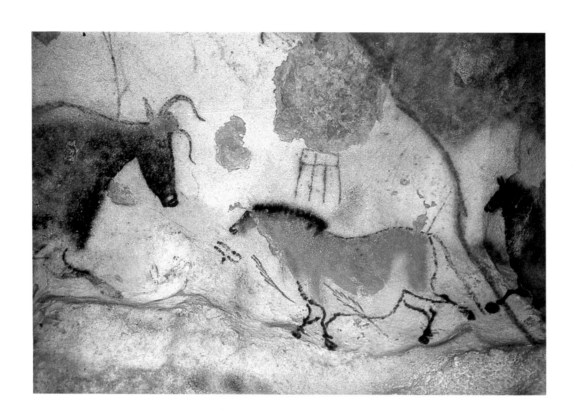

In the Caves of Auvergne

HE carved the red deer and the bull
  Upon the smooth cave rock,
Returned from war with belly full,
  And scarred with many a knock,
He carved the red deer and the bull
  Upon the smooth cave rock.

The stars flew by the cave's wide door,
  The clouds wild trumpets blew,
Trees rose in wild dreams from the floor,
  Flowers with dream faces grew
Up to the sky, and softly hung
  Golden and white and blue.

The woman ground her heap of corn,
  Her heart a guarded fire;
The wind played in his trembling soul
  Like a hand upon a lyre,
The wind drew faintly on the stone
  Symbols of his desire:

The red deer of the forests dark,
  Whose antlers cut the sky,
That vanishes into the mirk
  And like a dream flits by,
And by an arrow slain at last
  Is but the wind's dark body.

The bull that stands in marshy lakes
  As motionless and still
As a dark rock jutting from a plain
  Without a tree or hill;
The bull that is the sign of life,
  Its sombre, phallic will.

And from the dead white eyes of them
　　The wind springs up anew,
It blows upon the trembling heart,
　　And bull and deer renew
Their flitting life in the dim past
　　When that dead Hunter drew.

I sit beside him in the night,
　　And, fingering his red stone,
I chase through endless forests dark,
　　Seeking that thing unknown,
That which is not red deer or bull,
　　But which by them was shown:

By those stiff shapes in which he drew
His soul's exalted cry,
When flying down the forest dark,
　　He slew and knew not why,
When he was filled with song, and strength
　　Flowed to him from the sky.

The wind blows from red deer and bull,
　　The clouds wild trumpets blare,
Trees rise in wild dreams from the earth,
　　Flowers with dream faces stare;
O, *Hunter, your own shadow stands*
　　Within your forest lair!

W. J. Turner

THE next stage in man's relationship with animals, is the choice of an animal as the sacred symbol of a group; what is loosely called a totem. Hunting for their necessary food; and admiring to the point of worship a life-endowment greater than their own; there was thus established from the earliest times a dual relationship that has persisted to the present day: love and worship, enmity and fear.

Animals and Men, *Kenneth Clark*, 1977

Mountain Lion

CLIMBING through the January snow, into the Lobo canyon
Dark grow the spruce-trees, blue is the balsam, water
    sounds still unfrozen, and the trail is still evident.

Men!
Two men!
Men! The only animal in the world to fear!

They hesitate.
We hesitate.
They have a gun.
We have no gun.

Then we all advance, to meet.
Two Mexicans, strangers, emerging out of the dark
    and snow and inwardness of the Lobo valley.
What are you doing here on this vanishing trail?

What is he carrying?
Something yellow.
A deer?

Què tiene, amigo?
Lèon —

He smiles, foolishly, as if he were caught doing wrong.
And we smile, foolishly, as if we didn't know.
He is quite gentle and dark-faced.

It is a mountain lion,
A long, long slim cat, yellow like a lioness.
Dead.
He trapped her this morning, he says, smiling foolishly.

Lift up her face,
Her round, bright face, bright as frost.
Her round, fine-fashioned head, with two dead ears;
And stripes in the brilliant frost of her face, sharp, fine
    dark rays,
Dark, keen, fine eyes in the brilliant frost of her face.
Beautiful dead eyes.

Hermoso es!

They go out towards the open;
We go on into the gloom of Lobo.
And above the trees I found her lair,
A hole in the blood-orange brilliant rocks that stick up,
    a little cave.
And bones, and twigs, and a perilous ascent.

So, she will never leap up that way again, with the yellow
    flash of a mountain lion's long shoot!
And her bright striped frost-face will never watch any more,
    out of the shadow of the cave in the blood-orange rock,
Above the trees of the Lobo dark valley-mouth!

Instead, I look out.
And out to the dim of the desert, like a dream, never real;

To the snow of the Sangre de Cristo mountains, the ice
    of the mountains of Picoris,
And near across at the opposite steep of snow, green trees
    motionless standing in snow, like a Christmas toy.

And I think in this empty world there was room for me
    and a mountain lion.
And I think in the world beyond, how easily we might
    spare a million or two of humans

And never miss them.

Yet what a gap in the world, the missing white frost-face
  of that slim yellow mountain lion!

D. H. Lawrence

The Snare

I HEAR a sudden cry of pain!
   There is a rabbit in a snare:
Now I hear the cry again,
   But I cannot tell from where.

But I cannot tell from where
   He is calling out for aid;
Crying on the frightened air,
   Making everything afraid.

Making everything afraid,
   Wrinkling up his little face,
As he cries again for aid;
   And I cannot find the place!

And I cannot find the place
   Where his paw is in the snare:
Little one! Oh, little one!
   I am searching everywhere.

James Stephens

Hurt Hawks

THE broken pillar of the wing jags from the clotted shoulder,
The wing trails like a banner in defeat,
No more to use the sky forever but live with famine
And pain a few days: cat nor coyote
Will shorten the week of waiting for death, there is game without
talons.

He stands under the oak-bush and waits
The lame feet of salvation; at night he remembers freedom
And flies in a dream, the dawns ruin it.
He is strong and pain is worse to the strong, incapacity is worse.
The curs of the day come and torment him
At distance, no one but death the redeemer will humble that head,
The intrepid readiness, the terrible eyes.
The wild God of the world is sometimes merciful to those
That ask mercy, not often to the arrogant.
You do not know him, you communal people, or you have for-
gotten him;
Intemperate and savage, the hawk remembers him;
Beautiful and wild, the hawks, and men that are dying remember
him.

I'd sooner, except the penalties, kill a man than a hawk; but the
great redtail
Had nothing left but unable misery
From the bone too shattered for mending, the wing that trailed
under his talons when he moved.
We had fed him six weeks, I gave him freedom,
He wandered over the foreland hill and returned in the evening,
asking for death,
Not like a beggar, still eyed with the old
Implacable arrogance. I gave him the lead gift in the twilight.
What fell was relaxed,

Owl-downy, soft feminine feathers; but what
Soared: the fierce rush: the night-herons by the flooded river cried
fear at its rising
Before it was quite unsheathed from reality.

Robinson Jeffers

The Eagle

HE clasps the crag with crooked hands;
Close to the sun in lonely lands,
Ring'd with the azure world, he stands.

The wrinkled sea beneath him crawls;
He watches from his mountain walls,
And like a thunderbolt he falls.

Lord Tennyson

The Question

I DREAMED that, as I wandered by the way,
   Bare Winter suddenly was changed to Spring,
And gentle odours led my steps astray,
   Mixed with a sound of waters murmuring
Along a shelving bank of turf, which lay
   Under a copse, and hardly dared to fling
Its green arms round the bosom of the stream,
But kissed it and then fled, as thou mightest in dream.

There grew pied wind-flowers and violets,
   Daisies, those pearled Arcturi of the earth,
The constellated flower that never sets;
   Faint oxslips; tender bluebells, at whose birth
The sod scarce heaved; and that tall flower that wets —
   Like a child, half in tenderness and mirth —
Its mother's face with Heaven's collected tears,
When the low wind, its playmate's voice, it hears.

And in the warm hedge grew lush eglantine,
   Green cowbind and the moonlight-coloured may,
And cherry-blossoms, and white cups, whose wine
   Was the bright dew, yet drained not by the day;
And wild roses, and ivy serpentine,
   With its dark buds and leaves, wandering astray;
And flowers azure, black, and streaked with gold,
Fairer than any wakened eyes behold.

And nearer to the river's trembling edge
   There grew broad flag-flowers, purple pranked with white,
And starry river buds among the sedge,
   And floating water-lilies, broad and bright,
Which lit the oak that overhung the hedge
   With moonlight beams of their own watery light;

And bulrushes, and reeds of such deep green
As soothed the dazzled eye with sober sheen.

Methought that of these visionary flowers
   I made a nosegay, bound in such a way
That in the same hues, which in their natural bowers
   Were mingled or opposed, the like array
Kept these imprisoned children of the Hours
   Within my hand, — and then, elate and gay,
I hastened to the spot whence I had come,
That I might there present it! — Oh! to whom?

P. B. Shelley

Spring

Nothing is so beautiful as spring —
  When weeds, in wheels, shoot long and lovely and lush;
Thrush's eggs look little low heavens, and thrush
Through the echoing timber does so rinse and wring
The ear, it strikes like lightnings to hear him sing;
The glassy peartree leaves and blooms, they brush
The descending blue; that blue is all in a rush
With richness; the racing lambs too have fair their fling.

What is all this juice and all this joy?
A strain of the earth's sweet being in the beginning
In Eden garden. — Have, get, before it cloy,
Before it cloud, Christ, lord, and sour with sinning,
Innocent mind and Mayday in girl and boy,
Most, O maid's child, thy choice and worthy the winning.

Gerard Manley Hopkins

Pied Beauty

GLORY be to God for dappled things —
　　For skies of couple-colour as a brinded cow;
　　For rose-moles all in stipple upon trout that swim;
Fresh-firecoal chestnut-falls; finches' wings;
Landscape plotted and pieced - fold, fallow, and plough;
　　And áll trádes, their gear and tackle and trim.

All things counter, original, spare, strange;
　　Whatever is fickle, freckled (who knows how?)
　　　With swift, slow; sweet, sour, adazzle, dim;
He fathers-forth whose beauty is past change:
　　　　　　　　　　　　　Praise him.

Gerard Manley Hopkins

IMPERIOUSLY he leaps, he neighs, he bounds,
And now his woven girths he breaks asunder;
The bearing earth with his hard hoof he wounds;
Whose hollow womb resounds like heaven's thunder;
    The iron bit he crusheth 'tween his teeth,
    Controlling what he was controllèd with.

His ears up-prick'd; his braided hanging mane
Upon his compass'd crest now stand on end.
His nostrils drink the air, and forth again,
As from a furnace, vapours doth he send:
    His eye, which scornfully glisters like fire,
    Shows his hot courage and his high desire.

Round-hoof'd, short-jointed, fetlocks shag and long,
Broad breast, full eye, small head and nostril wide,
High crest, short ears, straight legs and passing strong,
Thin mane, thick tail, broad buttock, tender hide;
    Look, what a horse should have he did not lack,
    Save a proud rider on so proud a back.

from Venus and Adonis, *William Shakespeare*

Honorable Cat

I AM Cat.
   I am honorable.
I have pride.
I have dignity.
And I have a memory.
For I am older than you.
I am older than your Gods; the Tree Gods, the Stone Gods,
The Thunder and Lightning and the Sun Gods
And your God of Love.
I too can love
But with only half a heart
And that I offer you.
Accept what I am able to give
For were I to give you all
I could not bear your inevitable treachery.

Let us remain honorable friends.

Paul Gallico

The Span of Life

THE old dog barks backward without getting up,
I can remember when he was a pup.

Robert Frost

Cats Sleep Anywhere

CATS sleep
Anywhere,
Any table,
Any chair,
Top of piano,
Window-ledge,
In the middle,
On the edge,
Open drawer,
Empty shoe,
Anybody's
Lap will do,
Fitted in a
Cardboard box,
In the cupboard
With your frocks —
Anywhere!
They don't care!
Cats sleep
Anywhere.

Eleanor Farjeon

FREDERICK, Prince of Wales, father of King George III, was given a dog by Alexander Pope:

Engraved on the collar of a dog which I gave to
His Royal Highness:

I am his Highness' dog at Kew;
Pray tell me, sir, whose dog are you?

LOST in St James's Park, a little Spaniel Dog of his
Royal Highness; he will answer to the name *Towser*,
he is liver colour'd and white spotted, his legs speckled
with liver colour and white, with long hair growing upon
his hind legs, long ears, and his under lip a little hanging;
if any can give notice of him they shall have *five pounds*
for their pains.

from *The London Gazette*

The Owl and the Pussy-Cat

THE Owl and the Pussy-cat went to sea
　　In a beautiful pea-green boat,
They took some honey, and plenty of money,
　　Wrapped up in a five-pound note.
The Owl looked up to the stars above,
　　And sang to a small guitar,

'O lovely Pussy! O Pussy my love,
　　'What a beautiful Pussy you are,
　　　　'You are,
　　　　'You are!
'What a beautiful Pussy you are!'

Pussy said to the Owl, 'You elegant fowl!
　　'How charmingly sweet you sing!
'O let us be married! too long we have tarried:
　　'But what shall we do for a ring?'

They sailed away for a year and a day,
　　To the land where the Bong-tree grows,
And there in a wood a Piggy-wig stood,
　　With a ring at the end of his nose,
　　　　His nose,
　　　　His nose,
With a ring at the end of his nose.

'Dear Pig, are you willing to sell for one shilling
　　'Your ring?' Said the Piggy, 'I will.'
So they took it away, and were married next day
　　By the Turkey who lives on the hill.

They dined on mince, and slices of quince,
    Which they ate with a runcible spoon;
And hand in hand, on the edge of the sand,
    They danced by the light of the moon,
            The moon,
            The moon,
They danced by the light of the moon.

Edward Lear

The Pelican Chorus

King and Queen of the Pelicans we;
No other Birds so grand as we!
None but we have feet like fins!
With lovely leathery throats and chins!

    Ploffskin, Pluffskin, Pelican jee!
    We think no Birds so happy as we!
    Plumpskin, Ploshkin, Pelican jill!
    We think so then, and we thought so still!

We live on the Nile. The Nile we love.
By night we sleep on the cliffs above.
By day we fish, and at eve we stand
On long bare islands of yellow sand.
And when the sun sinks slowly down
And the great rock walls grow dark and brown,
Where the purple river rolls fast and dim
And the ivory Ibis starlike skim,
Wing to wing we dance around, —
Stamping our feet with a flumpy sound, —
Opening our mouths as Pelicans ought,
And this is the song we nightly snort:

    Ploffskin, Pluffskin, Pelican jee!
    We think no Birds so happy as we!
    Plumpskin, Ploshkin, Pelican jill!
    We think so then, and we thought so still.

Last year came out our Daughter Dell;
And all the Birds received her well.
To do her honour, a feast we made
For every bird that can swim or wade.
Herons and Gulls, and Cormorants black,

Cranes, and Flamingoes with scarlet back,
Plovers and Storks, and Geese in clouds,
Swans and Dilberry Ducks in crowds.
Thousands of Birds in wondrous flight!
They ate and drank and danced all night,
And echoing back from the rocks you heard
Multitude-echoes from Bird and Bird, —

Ploffskin, Pluffskin, Pelican jee!
We think no Birds so happy as we!
Plumpskin, Ploshkin, Pelican jill!
We think so then, and we thought so still!

Yes, they came; and among the rest,
The King of the Cranes all grandly dressed.
Such a lovely tail! Its feathers float
Between the ends of his blue dress-coat;
With pea-green trowsers all so neat,
And a delicate frill to hide his feet, —
(For though no one speaks of it, every one knows,
He had got no webs, between his toes!)
As soon as he saw our daughter Dell,
In violent love that Crane King fell, —
On seeing her waddling form so fair,
With a wreath of shrimps in her short white hair,
And before the end of the next long day,
Our Dell had given her heart away;
For the King of the Cranes had won that heart,
With a Crocodile's egg and a large fish-tart.
She vowed to marry the King of the Cranes,
Leaving the Nile for stranger plains;
And away they flew in a gathering crowd
Of endless birds in a lengthening cloud.

Ploffskin, Pluffskin, Pelican jee!
We think no Birds as happy as we!
Plumpkin, Ploshkin, Pelican jill!
We think so then, and we thought so still!

And far away in the twilight sky,
We heard them singing a lessening cry, —
Farther and farther till out of sight,
And we stood alone in the silent night!
Often since, in the nights of June,
We sit on the sand and watch the moon; -
She has gone to the great Gromboolian plain,
And we probably never shall meet again!
Oft, in the long still nights of June,
We sit on the rocks and watch the moon; -
She dwells by the the streams of the Chankly Bore,
And we probably never shall see her more.

Ploffskin, Pluffskin, Pelican jee!
We think no Birds so happy as we!
Plumpskin, Ploshkin, Pelican jill!
We think so then, and we thought so still!

Edward Lear

A Story about St Francis of Assisi

SOME years ago I went over to Italy to visit the Girl Guides of Monaco who were encamped in the countryside near a village called La Beccia, which lies between Arezzo and Florence.

The camp was on a meadow below the old monastery of La Verna, built in the thirteenth century to commemorate St Francis of Assisi receiving the Stigmata of of Christ. The monks had built a small chapel on the actual site, and every year on the anniversary they would leave the monastery at midnight to go in procession to the chapel where they had a special devotion to St Francis.

One year, because there was such a heavy blizzard with deep snow, it was impossible to have the procession. However, the following morning when the storm had subsided, the monks found in the thick snow the footprints of all the little animals who had gone up during the night to the chapel.

This story was told to me by the Franciscan monks at La Verna.

Princess Grace

St Francis and the Birds

WHEN Francis preached love to the birds
They listened, fluttered, throttled up
Into the blue like a flock of words

Released for fun from his holy lips.
Then wheeled back, whirred about his head,
Pirouetted on brothers' capes,

Danced on the wing, for sheer joy played
And sang, like images took flight.
Which was the best poem Francis made,

His argument true, his tone light.

Seamus Heaney

SAINT Francis of Assisi, do you remember
the sacred mountain, green above the lake,
  where first the vines and then the olives clamber,
  and flowers, so lulled with beauty, never wake —
    golden, crimson, blue,
  on the long drowsy terraces you loved and knew?

Still in the lake the painted island-town
  to the brown shelter of its Minster creeps,
  And still the kerchiefed boatman, bending down,
  scarce stirs the burnished water with his sweeps,
    and from the hill
  the monastery bell affirms your gospel still.

Your gospel of the birds and of the flowers,
  how every petal God has deigned to paint
  has by its sheer enamel all the powers,
  and more than all the beauty of the saint,
    and how the swallow
  worships with arrow flight that prayer is feign to follow

Your gospel of acceptance, that transposes
  God, and this earthly beauty He has made,
  finding the resurrection in the roses
  and all the angels in a single blade,
    and having heard
  the Twelve Apostles in the voice of a bird.

You sought no cloister, but with their wild-rose fire
  you built of understanding and of pardon
  the walls that shut out envy, hate, desire,
  or changed them into flowers in your garden,
    since all were part
  of the burden of man, and therefore, of *your heart*.

        from The Saint, *Humbert Wolfe*

36

Proud Songsters

THE thrushes sing as the sun is going,
    And the finches whistle in ones and pairs,
And as it gets dark loud nightingales
    In bushes
Pipe as they can when April wears,
As if all Time were theirs.

These are brand-new birds of twelve-months' growing,
Which a year ago, or less than twain,
No finches were, nor nightingales,
    Nor thrushes,
But only particles of grain,
    And earth, and air, and rain.

Thomas Hardy

A Bird's Epitaph

HERE lies a little bird,
  Once all day long
Through Martha's house was heard
His rippling song.

Tread lightly where he lies
  Beneath this stone
With nerveless wings, closed eyes,
And sweet voice gone.

Martin Armstrong

L̲AST night I was in the garden till 11 o'clock. It was the sweetest night that e're I saw. The garden looked so well and the roses and jasmine smelt beyond all perfume. And yet I was not pleased. The place had all the charms it used to have when I was most satisfied with it, — and had *you* been there I should have liked it much more than ever I did.

Dorothy Osborne, in a letter to Sir William Temple

Ask me no more where Jove bestows
When June is past, the fading rose;
For in your beauty's orient deep
These flowers, as in their causes, sleep.

Ask me no more whither do stray
The golden atoms of the day;
For in pure love Heaven did prepare
Those powders to enrich your hair.

Ask me no more whither doth haste
The nightingale when May is past,
For in your sweet dividing throat
She winters, and keeps warm her note.

Ask me no more when those stars' light
That downwards fall in dead of night;
For in your eyes they sit, and there
Fixed become as in their sphere.

Ask me no more if East or West
The phoenix builds her spicy nest;
For unto you at last she flies,
And in your fragrant bosom dies.

Thomas Carew

On a Rosebud sent to her Lover

THE tender bud within herself doth close
  With secret sweetness till it prove a rose;
And then as fit for profit as for pleasure
Yields sweet content to him that gains the treasure:

So she that sent this, yet a bud unblown,
In time may prove a rose, and be your own.

Anonymous seventeenth century

A Rose

A ROSE, as fair as ever saw the North,
  Grew in a little garden all alone;
A sweeter flower did Nature ne'er put forth,
Nor fairer garden yet was never known:
The maidens danced about it morn and noon,
And learned bards of it their ditties made;
The nimble fairies by the pale-faced moon
Water'd the root and kissed her pretty shade.
But well-a-day! — the gardener careless grew;
The maids and fairies both were kept away,
And in a drought the caterpillars threw
Themselves upon the bud and every spray.
  God shield the stock! If heaven send no supplies,
  The fairest blossom of the garden dies!

William Browne

CLAVDIO BRAVO. MCMLXII.

O how much more doth beauty beauteous seem
   By that sweet ornament which truth doth give!
The rose looks fair but fairer we it deem
For that sweet odour which doth in it live.
The canker-blooms have full as deep a dye
As the perfumed tincture of the roses
Hang on such thorns, and play as wantonly
When summer's breath their masked buds discloses,
But for their virtue only is their show
They live unwooed and unrespected fade;
Die to themselves, sweet roses do not so;
Of their sweet deaths are sweeter odours made. . . .

from Sonnet 54, *William Shakespeare*

THE damask rose is sweeter in the still than on the stalk while the distilled water of roses is good for strengthening the heart, and refreshing the spirits. The same put in junketting dishes, cakes, cordials, and many other pleasant things giveth a fine and most delectable taste.

A seventeenth century herbalist

Thoughts in a Garden

How vainly men themselves amaze
To win the palm, the oak, or bays,
And their uncessant labours see
Crown'd from some single herb or tree,
Whose short and narrow-verged shade
Does prudently their toils upbraid;
While all the flowers and trees do close
To weave the garlands of repose!

Fair Quiet, have I found thee here,
And Innocence thy sister dear?
Mistaken long, I sought you then
In busy companies of men:
Your sacred plants, if here below,
Only among the plants will grow:
Society is all but rude
To this delicious solitude.

No white nor red was ever seen
So amorous as this lovely green.
Fond lovers, cruel as their flame,
Cut in these trees their mistress' name:
Little, alas! they know or heed
How far these beauties hers exceed!
Fair trees! wheres'e'er your barks I wound,
No name but shall your own be found.

When we have run our passions' heat,
Love hither makes his best retreat:
The gods, that mortal beauty chase,
Still in a tree did end their race;
Apollo hunted Daphne so
Only that she might laurel grow;

And Pan did after Syrinx speed
Not as a nymph, but for a reed.

What wondrous life in this I lead!
Ripe apples drop about my head;
The luscious clusters of the vine
Upon my mouth do crush their wine;
The nectarine and curious peach
Into my hands themselves do reach;
Stumbling on melons, as I pass,
Ensnared with flowers, I fall on grass.

Meanwhile the mind from pleasure less
Withdraws into its happiness;
The mind, that Ocean where each kind
Does straight its own resemblance find;
Yet it creates, transcending these,
Far other worlds, and other seas;
Annihilating all that's made
To a green thought in a green shade.

Here at the fountain's sliding foot,
Or at some fruit-tree's mossy root,
Casting the body's vest aside,
My soul into the boughs does glide;
There, like a bird, it sits and sings,
Then whets and combs its silver wings,
And, till prepared for longer flight,
Waves in its plumes the various light.

Such was that happy Garden-state
While man there walk'd without a mate:
After a place so pure and sweet,
What other help could yet be meet!
But 'twas beyond a mortal's share

To wander solitary there:
Two paradises 'twere in one,
To live in Paradise alone.

How well the skilful gard'ner drew
Of flowers and herbs this dial new!
Where, from above, the milder sun
Does through a fragrant zodiac run:
And, as it works, th'industrious bee
Computes its time as well as we.
How could such sweet and wholesome hours
Be reckon'd, but with herbs and flowers!

Andrew Marvell

Binsey Poplars
(felled 1879)

My aspens dear, whose airy cages quelled,
  Quelled or quenched in leaves the leaping sun,
All felled, felled, are all felled;
  Of a fresh and following folded rank
        Not spared, not one
        That dandled a sandalled
      Shadow that swam or sank
On meadow and river and wind-wandering
  weed-winding bank.

O if we but knew what we do
      When we delve or hew –
    Hack and rack the growing green!
        Since country is so tender
    To touch, her being só slender,
    That, like this sleek and seeing ball
    But a prick will make no eye at all,
    Where we, even where we mean
        To mend her we end her,
      When we hew or delve:
After-comers cannot guess the beauty been.
    Ten or twelve, only ten or twelve
      Strokes of havoc únselve
        The sweet especial scene,
      Rural scene, a rural scene,
      Sweet especial rural scene.

Gerard Manley Hopkins

The Redwoods

MOUNTAINS are moving, rivers
are hurrying. But we
are still.

We have the thoughts of giants —
clouds, and at night the stars.

And we have names — guttural, grotesque —
Hamet, Og — names with no syllables.

And perish, one by one, our roots
gnawed by the mice. And fall.

And are too slow for death, and change
to stone. Or else too quick,

like candles in a fire. Giants
are lonely. We have waited long

for someone. By our waiting, surely
there must be someone at whose touch

our boughs would bend; and hands
to gather us; a spirit

to whom we are light as the hawthorn tree.
O if there is a poet

let him come now! We stand at the Pacific
like great unmarried girls,

turning in our heads the stars and clouds,
considering whom to please.

Louis Simpson

I THINK I could turn and live with animals, they are so
placid and self-contained,
I stand and look at them long and long.

They do not sweat and whine about their condition;
They do not lie awake in the dark and weep for their sins;
They do not make me sick discussing their duty to God;
Not one is dissatisfied, not one is demented with the mania
of owning things
Not one kneels to another, nor to his kind that lived
thousands of years ago;
Not one is respectable or unhappy over the whole earth.

from Song of Myself, *Walt Whitman*

THERE be four things which are little upon the earth
But they are exceeding wise;
The ants are a people not strong,
Yet they prepare their meat in the summer;
The conies are but a feeble folk,
Yet they make their houses in the rocks;
The locusts have no king,
Yet they go forth all of them by bands;
The spider taketh hold with her hands,
And is in kings' palaces.

COME into animal presence.
No man is so guileless as
the serpent. The lonely white
rabbit on the roof is a star
twitching its ears at the rain.
The llama intricately
folding its hind legs to be seated
not distains but mildly
disregards human approval.
What joy when the insouciant
armadillo glances at us and doesn't
quicken his trotting
across the track into the palm brush.
What is this joy? That no animal
falters, but knows what it must do?
That the snake has no blemish,
that the rabbit inspects his strange surroundings
in white star-silence? The llama
rests in dignity, the armadillo
has some intention to pursue in the palm forest.
Those who were sacred have remained so,
holiness does not dissolve, it is a presence
of bronze, only the sight that saw it
faltered, and turned from it.
An old joy returns in holy presence.

Denise Levertov

The Heaven of Animals

HERE they are. The soft eyes open.
If they have lived in a wood
It is a wood.

If they have lived on plains
It is grass rolling
Under their feet forever.

Having no souls they have come,
Anyway, beyond their knowing.
Their instincts wholly bloom
And they rise.
The soft eyes open.

To match them, the landscape flowers,
Outdoing, desperately
Outdoing what is required:
The richest wood
The deepest field.

For some of these.
It could not be the place
It is, without blood.
These hunt, as they have done,
But with claws and teeth grown perfect.

More deadly than they can believe.
They stalk more silently,
And crouch on the limbs of trees,
And their descent
Upon the bright backs of their prey
May take years
In a soveriegn floating of joy.

And those that are hunted
Know this as their life,
Their reward: to walk
Under such trees in full knowledge
Of what is in glory above them,
And to feel no fear,
But acceptance, compliance.
Fulfilling themselves without pain

At the cycle's centre,
They tremble, they walk
Under the tree,
They fall, they are torn,
They rise, they walk again.

James Dickey

HE sendeth the springs into the valleys, which run among the hills.

They give drink to every beast of the field: the wild asses quench their thirst.

By them shall the fowls of the heaven have their habitation, which sing among the branches.

He causeth the grass to grow for the cattle, and herb for the service of man: that he may bring forth food out of the earth.

The trees of the Lord are full of sap; the cedars of Lebanon, which he hath planted;

Where the birds make their nests: as for the stork, the fir trees are her house.

The high hills are a refuge for the wild goats; and the rocks for the conies.

He appointed the moon for seasons: the sun knoweth his going down. . . .

Thou makest darkness, and it is night: wherein all the beasts of the forest do creep forth.

O LORD, how manifold are thy
works! in wisdom hast thou made
them all: the earth is full of thy
riches.

from Psalm 104

Illustrations

Frontispiece   Flower Arrangement - Princess Grace of Monaco

Facing page 2   The Animals Going into the Ark - Studio of Bassano, 16th century. By Gracious Permission of Her Majesty Queen Elizabeth the Queen Mother.

7   Humming Birds - John James Audubon (1785-1851). By permission of the New York Historical Society.

8   Tyger - Fleur Cowles. By courtesy of the Artist.

11   Horse and Bull - Paleolithic Cave Painting c. 20,000 BC. By courtesy of M. Jean Vertut.

18   Hawks - John James Audubon. By permission of the New York Historical Society

24   Turkish Groom holding an Arab Stallion - C. Vernet. Collection of Mr and Mrs Paul Mellon.

26   The Ides of March - Andrew Wyeth. Copyright 1974 by Andrew Wyeth. Private Collection.

28   Miss Jane Bowles 1775 - Sir Joshua Reynolds (1723-92). By courtesy of the Trustees of the Wallace Collection.

30   Cat - Claudio Bravo. By courtesy of the Artist, collection Fleur Cowles.

33   The Pelican - Edward Lear. By courtesy of Weidenfeld and Nicolson and the Linnaeus Society.

39   Roses - Graham Sutherland (1903-80), collection Fleur Cowles.

42   Rosebud - Claudio Bravo. By courtesy of the Artist, collection Fleur Cowles.

45   The Greenhouse, Woodside House, Berkshire - Thomas Robins. By courtesy of Major and Mrs J. B. Ford.

48   Poplars 1981 - Andrew Gemmill. By courtesy of the Artist. Private Collection.

52   Llamas - Waterhouse Hawkins version. By courtesy of Weidenfeld and Nicolson and the Linnaeus Society.

53   The Heaven of Animals - Jan Brueghel the Velvet. By permission of the Louvre.

Acknowledgments

The publishers would like to acknowledge the help of the many authors, publishers and agents who have given permission for the reproduction of poetry and prose in this anthology. A summary of these, with brief notes by John Carroll on some of the authors, is given below in the order in which their works appear in the book.

from *Auguries of Innocence* and *The Tyger*
William Blake (1757-1827). Poet, mystic and artist. Born in London the son of a hosier, he did not go to school but was apprenticed to James Basire, engraver to the Society of Antiquaries. In 1789 he engraved and published his *Songs of Innocence*, in which he first showed the mystical cast of his mind. The *Auguries of Innocence* were written about 1803, and consist of 137 stanzas. *The Tyger* comes from the *Songs of Experience*, published in 1794.

The History of the Flood
(by permission of David Higham Associates)
John Heath-Stubbs, born 1918 in London. He has held the Gregory Fellowship in Poetry at Leeds University and Visiting Professorships of English in Egypt and the U.S.A. His *Selected Poems* received the Arts Council award and his long poem *Artorius* gained him the Queen's Gold Medal for Poetry.

from *Miracles* and from *Song of Myself*
Walt Whitman (1819-1892). His mother's people were Dutch Quakers. On his father's side he was descended from English Puritans who had farmed American soil for a century and a half. Whitman set himself the Atlantean task of uplifting into the sphere of poetry the whole of modern life and man, omitting nothing, concealing nothing.

Humming Bird and *Mountain Lion*
David Herbert Lawrence (1885-1930) was born in a Nottinghamshire mining village, his father a coal-miner. He gave up teaching to devote himself to writing and after *Sons and Lovers* (1913) became one of the outstanding novelists of the time. His poems echo the passionate struggle of his spirit, vivid and often compassionate.

In those Tropical Forests . . .
Mary Kingsley (1862-1900) was a niece of the novelist Charles Kingsley. She was an enterprising traveller in West Africa between 1893 and 1899. She wrote *Travels in West Africa*, published in 1896, and died a nurse in a South African hospital during the Boer war. She was an ardent advocate of a better understanding between the black and white races.

The Babiaantje
(by permission of Anvil Press Poetry)
F. T. Prince, born 1912 in South Africa. He was educated there and at Oxford and Princeton Universities. He has been Professor of English at Southampton University, a Visiting Fellow at All Souls, Oxford, and more recently Professor of English at the University of the West Indies and Visiting Professor at St Louis University in the United States.

Animals and Men (two extracts)
(by courtesy of William Morrow and Thames and Hudson)
Kenneth Clark (born 1903). Lord Clark of Saltwood, O.M., C.H., K.C.B. One of our most distinguished authorities on the arts of painting, sculpture and kindred subjects. Also very well known to the general public for his brilliant television series *Civilisation*.

In the Caves of the Auvergne
(by courtesy of Sidgwick and Jackson)
W. J. Turner (1889-1946). Born in Melbourne, Australia. Served in the Royal Artillery 1916-18. He succeeded Siegfried Sassoon as Literary Editor of the *Daily Herald*. Novelist, essayist, and a poet of great range and strength.

The Snare
(by permission of Macmillan)
James Stephens (1883-1950). Born in Dublin, many of his poems and stories have a strong Irish flavour. He was also well known as a delightful broadcaster for the BBC.

Hurt Hawks
(by permission of Random House)
Robinson Jeffers (1887-1962). Born in Pittsburgh, he travelled extensively as a child with his parents in Europe. Returning to America at the age of fifteen, he and his family settled in California. It was to become his permanent home and he identified

himself with the Californian rocks and headlands on the ocean's edge. His poetry communicates a stormy vigour. It never falters, but sweeps on, cumulative and irresistible.

The Eagle
Alfred Tennyson (1809-1892). He was born at Somersby, Lincolnshire, the fourth of the rector's eight sons. He was appointed *poet laureate* in succession to Wordsworth, in November 1850. In 1884 he was created first Baron Tennyson. He died 6th October 1892, and was buried in Westminster Abbey.

The Question
Percy Bysshe Shelley, born 4th August 1792 at Field Place, near Horsham in Sussex. Drowned at sea in the bay of Spezzia on 8th July 1822. Shelley's body was consumed by fire on the beach in the presence of Byron, Leigh Hunt and Trelawny. The ashes subsequently being buried in the Protestant cemetery at Rome, close to where John Keats had already been interred. *The Question* was included in *Posthumous Poems*, 1824.

Spring, *Pied Beauty* and *Binsey Poplars - felled* 1879
Gerard Manley Hopkins (1844-1889) became a Jesuit priest in 1877. His poems, mostly written after 1875, were first published in 1918 by Robert Bridges, to whose care Hopkins had entrusted them. A few years later, their power and technique considerably influenced a new generation of poets.

from *Venus and Adonis* and from *Sonnet 54*
William Shakespeare (1564-1616). *Venus and Adonis* was published in 1593. Shakespeare, in the dedication to the Earl of Southampton, calls it 'the first heir of my invention', which may mean the first of his works to be written, or the first to be published. Francis Meres testified to the poem's popularity in his *Palladis Tamia*, 1598: 'So the sweete wittie soule of *Ouid* lives in mellifluous & hony-tongued *Shakespeare*, witnes his *Venus* and *Adonis*, his *Lucrece*, his sugred Sonnets among his private friends . . .'

Honorable Cat
(by permission of Crown Publishers and Hughes Massie)
Paul Gallico (1897-1976). Author and journalist. Many of his novels were adapted for the cinema. *Honorable Cat* is the title poem for a collection of verses about cats.

The Span of Life
(by permission of Holt Rinehart & Winston and Jonathan Cape)
Robert Frost (1874-1963). Often regarded as the chief interpreter of New England, he was born in San Francisco, California. He studied at Harvard and between 1900 and 1905 he farmed in New Hampshire. In 1913 his book, *A Boy's Will*, was published in England when he was thirty-nine. He had sold his farm, gone to London and made friends with Edward Thomas and other English poets and writers. In 1914, his collection of poems, *North of Boston*, was also published in England. The following year he returned to America where *North of Boston* had been reprinted. Its author, who had left the country an unknown writer, returned to find himself famous. In succeeding years numerous honours, degrees and prizes were awarded to him and he became America's unofficial poet laureate. His poetry was an early influence on the painter Andrew Wyeth.

Cats Sleep Anywhere
(by permission of David Higham Associates)
Eleanor Farjeon (1881-1965). Although best known as a writer of children's stories and verse, she also wrote a vivid and moving book of memoirs about her friendship with the poet Edward Thomas.

'I am his Highness' dog at Kew . . .'
Alexander Pope (1688-1744). He was born in London, the son of a Lombard Street linen-draper. As a boy, hardly above ten years old, he learnt, says Dr Johnson, to take Dryden as his model; and was 'impressed with such veneration for his instructor, that he persuaded some friends to take him to the coffee-house which Dryden frequented, and pleased himself with having seen him.' Wycherley introduced the young poet to London life, where he soon established a friendship with Addison, Steele and Swift. His *Essay on Criticism* 1711, placed him in the front rank of men of letters of his time.

The Owl and The Pussycat and *The Pelican Chorus*
Edward Lear (1812-1888). Artist, author, traveller and art-teacher to Queen Victoria. He has won a place unique in English literature for his fantastic and delightful nonsense verses. He died at San Remo, on the Italian Riviera, where he had lived for many years.

St Francis and the Birds, from *Death of a Naturalist*
(reprinted by permission of Faber and Faber)
Seamus Heaney, born 1939 in Co. Derry, Northern Ireland.
He grew up in the country in touch with a traditional way of
life that he wrote about in his first book, *Death of a Naturalist*,
1966. Since then he has had six books published, the most re-
cent *Selected Poems*, 1980 establishing him as a poet of major
distinction.

from *The Saint*
(by kind permission of Ann Wolfe)
Humbert Wolfe (1885-1940). Born in Milan and brought up
in Yorkshire. He was educated at Bradford Grammar School
and Wadham College, Oxford. His career lay in the Civil Ser-
vice where he achieved great distinction. His first book, *London
Sonnets* was published in 1920 and during the next twenty years
he wrote, or edited, more than forty books.

Proud Songsters
Thomas Hardy (1840-1928). When he published his first
novel, *Desperate Remedies*, in 1871, he had already written
some thirty poems. After his last novel, *Jude the Obscure* 1896,
he began to publish his poetry with *Wessex Poems* 1898. By
1922 he had produced a large number of lyric and narrative
poems. *Proud Songsters* comes from the posthumous collection
of poems called *Winter Words* published the year of his death.

A Bird's Epitaph
(reprinted by permission of A. D. Peters and Co. Ltd.)
Martin Armstrong (1882-1974). Poet, novelist and short-story
writer. Also author of a volume of reminiscences of his child-
hood called *Victorian Peep-Show*.

'*Last night I was in the Garden* . . .' from a letter to Sir William
Temple
Dorothy Osborne (1627-1695). Daughter of a royalist, Sir
Peter Osborne, who did not favour her marrying William
Temple because his father was a member of the Long Parlia-
ment. The lovers were constant in their affection, and their
seven years of separation gave opportunity for Dorothy's de-
lightful letters. They were eventually married in 1654.

Ask Me No More
Thomas Carew (pronounced 'Carey'), born c. 1598-1639.
Travelled in embassies to Venice, Turin, and France. He wrote

a fine elegy on John Donne and numerous graceful songs and lyrics.

A Rose
William Browne (c. 1590-1643) was a follower of Spenser, particularly noted for his pastoral poetry in *The Shepheards Pipe* 1614 and his three volumes *Britannia's Pastorals* 1613-1625. He was an Oxford graduate and studied at the Inns of Court (his *Inner Temple Masque* being performed in January 1615). He took service with the Earl of Pembroke and one of his most well-known pieces is his epitaph on the Countess.

Thoughts in a Garden
Andrew Marvell (1621-1678). The son of a clergyman, master of the Almhouse at Hull, Marvell was educated at Hull Grammar School and Trinity College, Cambridge. In 1651 he became tutor to the daughter of Lord Fairfax, the victor of the battle of Naseby. In 1653, John Milton recommended him to be his assistant in the Latin Secretaryship under the Lord Protector, Oliver Cromwell. As a Member of Parliament for Hull from 1659 until his death, Marvell was a staunch defender of constitutional liberties.

The Redwoods
(by permission of Wesleyan University Press. Copyright 1961) Louis Simpson, born 1923 in Jamaica, went to the United States in 1940 where he attended Columbia University. He spent three years in the U.S. Army. He has been a publisher and has taught at the Universities of California, Berkeley and at Stony Brook in Long Island.

'There be four things . . .' and from *Psalm 104*
The King James Bible, or the 'Authorised Version' as it is also called, was the result of a conference at Hampton Court Palace convened by King James I in 1604. The revisers were forty-seven in number and were drawn from the most eminent scholars and divines of the day. The work of revision and retranslation occupied three and a half years, the result being first published in 1611.

'Come into animal presence' from *The Jacobs Ladder*
(by permission of New Directions and Laurence Pollinger Ltd) Denise Levertov, born 1923 in Ilford, Essex. She served as a nurse during the Second World War when some of her poems were first published. She married the American writer, Mitchell Goodman, and has lived in the United States since 1948.

The Heaven of Animals from *Drowning with Others*
(by permission of Wesleyan University Press)
James Dickey, born 1923 in Georgia, U.S.A. He has been a
Guggenheim Fellow, consultant in poetry for the Library of
Congress, and teaches at the University of South Carolina.

The publishers would like to thank the following in addition
to those already mentioned:

Phyllis Earl, James N. Sicks, Beverley Carter, Margaret
Murphy, The le Fevre Gallery, Mary Alice Kennedy, Beatrice
Phillpotts, Jane Kaufmann, Gwyn Westbury-Jones, Colin
Webb, Joan Culham, Margaret Vines, Anne Sydney, Paul
Hutton, Bonnie Prandato, Katia Gould.